Multi-Industry Success Stories
Healthcare, Tax Administration, Government, Professional Services, and Nonprofit

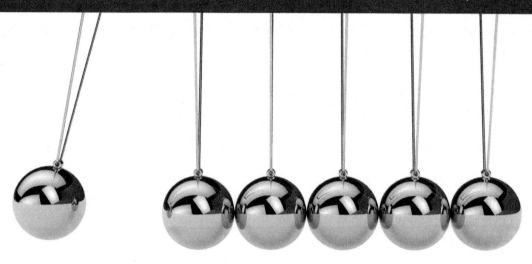

CLEAR
COMMUNICATION
WITH CLEAR RESULTS

How to start a plain language program
where you work

Center for Plain Language
——— Make it clear ———

Clear Communication with Clear Results: How to Start a Plain Language Program Where You Work

Published by Center for Plain Language • 21 East Main Street • Richmond VA 23219

Executive Editor: Donna M. Creason
Editorial Team: Brian Berkenstock, Robin Kilroy, Beth Landau, Lisa Van Alstyne, Pat Truman
Cover Design: Anurup Ghosh @ 99designs
Interior Layout: Flipside Production

CONTENTS

ICONS USED IN THIS EBOOK

Each organization's story follows the same sequence of questions. The following icons can help you jump into whichever section of a story is most useful to you.

Identifiable Problem

Every good tale starts with a hearty challenge. Scan this section to see which story most resembles your own.

Specific Goals

Our heroes dream of a better future. Will they make the dream come true?

Actions

Rich with detail, this part of our story reveals strategies and tactics.

Problems, Obstacles, or Challenges

The plot thickens as our heroes face challenges and opposition.

Progress

See how to avoid pitfalls, secure support and build a strong team and process.

Outcomes

This is the big finish. Find out if our heroes succeeded in their journey.

INTRODUCTION

Somewhere along the way, the world view on clear communication shifted. For government, nonprofits, and the private sector, clear communication was no longer simply a "nice to have," something done as if for charity. The work of clear communication is now expected. It's the norm. Organizations that don't deliver can fall by the wayside, lose funding, and see support disappear.

How did we get to this tipping point?

Some demand came from the people. The digital explosion, in particular, placed a high value on good customer service. You simply can't deliver that without clarity: clarity of word, design, and experience.

Some demand came from the law, like the Plain Writing Act of 2010. (We're proud to say the Center had a hand in that.) Accessibility laws also played a part. The disability community grew tired of being ignored. They organized, rose up, and demanded their rights.

And **some demand came from you**, professionals from…

- ⇒ Accessibility
- ⇒ Branding
- ⇒ Communications
- ⇒ Design
- ⇒ Information technology
- ⇒ Marketing
- ⇒ Search engine optimization
- ⇒ User experience

You have long known that clear communication—in all its fullness of organization and structure, logic and sentences, and word choice—is right, sensible, and the way things should be. Your diligence in pushing the need to always be clear helped drive the change.

Center for Plain Language

What's In This Book?

In these pages you'll hear from five organizations that share the Center's vision:

Create a culture of clarity
Every audience ▪ Every format ▪ Every time

I have seen many organizations announce a "simplification" or plain language program. A limitation for many was that they thought "plain language" meant only getting employees to use simple words and short sentences. As a result, they easily abandoned the work when the need to communicate technical details arose or when experts or executives needed to write (as if experts and executives are barred from communicating clearly).

In contrast, the five organizations featured in this e-book have created serious programs or initiatives to deliver clear communication. They have embedded clear communication into the fabric of their organizations. We hope you'll find within the pages of this e-book many ideas to try where you work or with your clients. We believe you will succeed.

Enjoy!

Susan Kleimann

Susan Kleimann, Ph.D.
Chair, Center for Plain Language
President, Kleimann Communication Group

DO YOU HAVE A STORY TO SHARE?
Help us build Volume 2. You can reach us at
centerforplainlanguage@gmail.com.

Center for Plain Language

A BRIEF HISTORY OF THE CENTER

In the mid-1990s, a group of federal plain language advocates met monthly in Washington DC. They first called themselves PEN, for the Plain English Network. In 2000, they became PLAIN, for the Plain Language Action and Information Network.

In the early 2000s, five people—Annetta Cheek, Joe Kimble, Susan Kleimann, Joanne Locke, and Ginny Redish—created a new group of communicators from all walks of life: academics, consultants, healthcare organizations, and the business community. This was the birth of the Center.

In 2003, the Center for Plain Language was formed as a 501c3 nonprofit. Their goal? Help government agencies and businesses write so clearly to their audiences that everyone understands what they are reading the first time they read it.

In the thirteen years of its existence, the Center has enjoyed a host of accomplishments:

- Trained people through workshops
- Cosponsored two international conferences
- Advocated the passage of the Plain Writing Act of 2010 (success!)
- Advocated for the passage of the Plain Regulations Act (not yet…)
- Graded government writing with annual Report Cards
- Celebrated good writing with the ClearMark Awards
- Raised awareness by spotlighting not-so-good writing with the WonderMark Awards

If this sounds like your kind of place, become a member. And spread the word to your colleagues and management about the benefits of a membership. (For example, this e-book is free when you join!)

Center for Plain Language

TOP 10 LIST OF GUIDING PRINCIPLES

The following list includes recurring insights culled from the five case studies presented in this e-book as well as some unique, and enlightening, tidbits from individual contributors.

10 **Get support from top execs.** Let's be honest. This is the best way to get things done. Commitment from the top makes every step in the process of building a clear communication program easier. When faced with opposition to change, you can say, "Well, if you want to go against the wishes of the CEO…" (Then watch the verbal backtracking and acrobatics that ensue to get out of that one!)

9 **Become the expert.** Don't wait for someone higher up on the org chart to start the process. *You* become the expert. Then, find like-minded crusaders and band together. Employees look to experts to make key decisions. Most people are not opposed to hearing, "This is the new way." In fact, knowing the "rules" can simplify their lives. It gives them an authority to reference when faced with questions or opposition.

8 **Convert coworkers.** Whether you start with top support or build from the grassroots up, you'll need to educate colleagues so they'll join you. Appeal to their common sense ("Clear communication is good for everyone.") and their desire for success. ("Being at the forefront of this movement will make you look goooood.") You may have to build relationships one at a time. Will you convince everyone? No, but you'll eventually tip the balance in favor of clear communication.

7 **Keep up the momentum.** Always recognize and reward people who join the team, support the new or growing program and who produce good work. A simple e-mail (with a cc to a manager) can mean so much.

6 **Train. Train. Train.** It's not fair to ask people to change without giving them the tools they need. So offer in-person or virtual workshops. Create self-guided digital courses. Publish a newsletter or share e-mails with tips and tricks. (Outreach serves a dual purpose: you're also keeping people engaged for the long haul.)

5 **Be patient.** It may take time. Maybe more than you expected. (As in, your "worst-case-scenario" amount of time!) It's easy to give up. Don't. Instead, take a breather. Ask for help. Share the load.

Center for Plain Language

4 **Assume positive intent.** At times, it may seem like people are trying to block your common-sense, verifiable practices of clear communication. These folks are not evil. Some need an education to open their eyes about the proven value of clear communication. Others are on autopilot, saying "no" to any change. Yours is just the latest one. No one is actively against being clear. Or helping people. (OK. We're not sure about the DMV, but we remain ever hopeful.) Assume everyone wants to support clear communication. Your job is to help them get there.

3 **Tailor your pitch to your audience.** Every sales leader knows you need to find out what your buyer values most. People in branding and marketing love to hear about "connecting with consumers." Clear communication does that. User experience experts want to create the smoothest journey possible. Yep, clear communication can help. Executives love "thought leadership." Entice them to be a leader rather than a follower with clear communication. Finance folks want a "return on investment." Show them the dramatic increase in search engine optimization that follows a plain language overhaul.

2 **It's about more than words.** The Center for Plain Language is sometimes hindered by its historical name. But obviously, clear communication is about more than words. So when you build your program, recruit supporters from the fields that need clear communication to succeed: advertising, branding, customer service, design, information technology, marketing, search engine optimization, and user experience, among many others.

1 **Be joyful.** This one might sounds a bit corny. But making life easier for people feels pretty darn good. And that's the greatest gift clear communication delivers. You also get to work on something you believe in. Not everyone can say that. Plus, you'll meet a ton of awesome people who share your passion. So have fun. Celebrate your wins. Use humor when you have to commiserate about challenges. And be sure to look back at the work that you complete so you can marvel at the improvements and accomplishments.

Center for Plain Language

Aetna is a leading healthcare benefits company, providing information and resources to help people make better informed decisions about their healthcare and the financial side of healthcare. Approximately 50,000 people call Aetna "my employer." And about 46 million people rely on Aetna to help them make decisions about their healthcare and their healthcare spending. Aetna products include medical, pharmacy, dental, behavioral health, group life, and disability plans. They also offer services for healthcare management, workers' compensation administration, and health information technology.

An interview with...

Vicki Lankarge
Marketing Director and one of the architects of
Aetna's Plain Language Initiative

www.aetna.com

IDENTIFIABLE PROBLEM

What was the catalyst for Aetna to consider instituting a plain language program?

Because Aetna is a healthcare company, it makes sense that its foray into plain language and clear communication started with health literacy. Long before "plain language" made it into the vernacular at this Fortune 50 company, Aetna had a Health Literacy Workgroup.

Composed of a medical director, communications executive, two quality managers, a marketer, and an editor, the workgroup sought to educate the company about the critical issue of poor health literacy.

The National Assessment of Adult Literacy—a 2003 survey that spurred the group into action—found nearly nine out of ten adults had trouble understanding and using health information. The workgroup connected with like-minded writers and proofreaders across the company who all faced a constant battle: getting everyone at Aetna who created or reviewed consumer-facing materials to communicate clearly.

A handful of editorial types already knew the value of using plain language and delivering content that was simple and clear and that tested well with real people.

"So we had proof, both internal and external, to support our efforts," says Vicki Lankarge, a marketing director and one of the architects of Aetna's plain language initiative. "We just had to convince people that change was needed—for a host of good reasons."

 ## SPECIFIC GOALS

Describe what Aetna's goals were for the program.

The first goal of the growing team was to create awareness.

"Nothing changes until people know there's a problem," says Carla Espinoza, one of the founding members of the workgroup. "We shared *Before & After* examples, which are a dramatic way to show people the huge improvement good writing and design can have."

 Center for Plain Language

Before

Dear Member:

On March 30, 2007, the Food and Drug Administration (FDA) announced that Novartis Pharmaceuticals Corporation has agreed to stop marketing Zelnorm® (tegaserod).[1] A study of patients taking Zelnorm found that there may be an increased risk of heart attack, chest pain and stroke associated with use of the drug. Novartis agreed to withdraw Zelnorm in the United States until more research can be done.[2]

What you should do
If you or anyone in your household is currently taking Zelnorm, please talk to your physician right away about using a different drug instead.[3] Zelnorm will no longer be available at pharmacies. It also will not be covered under your Aetna prescription plan.[4]

Refunds for unused Zelnorm
You can return any unused and unexpired Zelnorm tablets to Novartis for a refund of out-of-pocket costs. To learn more, you can call Novartis, the maker of Zelnorm, at 1-888-NOW-NOVA (1-888-669-6682), or visit their website, www.zelnorm.com.

Questions about Zelnorm
Talk with your doctor. He or she can help you find other treatments that Aetna covers.[5]

The FDA has a Zelnorm information website at www.fda.gov/cder/drug/infopage/zelnorm/default.htm.[6]

Please contact us with any questions you might have about your prescription benefits at the toll-free number on your member ID card. You can log on to Aetna Navigator™, your secure member website, at www.aetna.com.

We hope this information is helpful. Your health and safety are important to us.

Sincerely,

Reading Grade Level: 10.1

footnote

1 This sentence is long – 22 words – and crammed with large words. The reading grade level is 18.1.

2 Readers may not understand that "Novartis agreed to withdraw Zelnorm" means the drug will no longer be sold.

3 This sentence has a reading grade level of 12.9. Why? It's long and uses many multisyllabic words – "anyone," "currently," "physician," "different."

4 This information is valuable. It is moved to the first paragraph in the revised letter.

5 This information is included in the revised letter, but in different places.

6 This sentence is improved in two ways: 1) The new text is active – "Learn more…" – instead of passive – "The FDA has…" 2) The new text cut the words "information" and "website." (Readers know that a URL means "website." And they know that "Learn more" implies "information.")

After

Dear Member:

People who take Zelnorm® may be at an increased risk of heart attack, chest pain and stroke.[7] This news comes from a recent study. For this reason, the drug will no longer be sold in the United States. Pharmacies will no longer carry Zelnorm. And it will not be covered under your Aetna plan.[8]

What you should do
Talk to your doctor right away if you take this drug. Your doctor can help you find other treatments that Aetna covers.[9]

How to get a refund
You can return your unused Zelnorm to Novartis. You will be refunded for your out-of-pocket costs. Call 1-888-NOW-NOVA (1-888-669-6682). Or visit www.zelnorm.com.[10]

Where to find more information
Learn more about Zelnorm at: www.fda.gov/cder/drug/infopage/zelnorm/default.htm.

Do you have questions about your prescription benefits? Call the toll-free number on your member ID card. Or log on to Aetna Navigator™ at www.aetna.com.[11]

We hope this information is helpful. Your health and safety are important to us.

Sincerely,

Reading Grade Level: 4.8

footnote

7 The revised text puts the most important message first: "This drug is dangerous." The new text cuts out less important facts, such as the name of the drug maker and that the FDA made the announcement.

8 The revised paragraph lays out the important message in an order that's logical from the reader's point of view: 1) This drug you take is dangerous. 2) A new study tells us this. 3) Because it's dangerous, this drug will no longer be sold. 4) This means pharmacies won't carry it and Aetna will not pay for it. The new paragraph uses smaller words and shorter sentences. It has a reading grade level of 4.3; the original paragraph scored 12.4.

9 The revised text contains the same message as the original version, but the new version uses two sentences instead of one. It also uses smaller words: "doctor" instead of "physician" and "other" instead of "different."

10 Note: When calculating reading grade level, skip phone numbers and web addresses. The readability tool in Microsoft Word can't account for this text.

11 The original text was made of two sentences. One sentence contained two commas. (Commas raise the reading grade level. This doesn't mean you should never use commas, but if the sentence can be changed to avoid them, do so.) Also, when breaking long sentences into shorter ones, don't be afraid to start a sentence with "or," "and" or "but." These are acceptable when you write the way you speak. And that's the style we're using in our communication with members.

Figure 1. The well-received Before & After letter to customers telling them that a prescription drug they used was being discontinued

"The original letter had that officious tone that many companies use," says Brian Berkenstock, director of content strategy at bswift, an Aetna company. "It's that old-school, stuffy tone that says, 'We want to sound important and we know more than you.' Just awful stuff to foist on people who really just need to know why you're contacting them and what you want them to do."

"The original letter was crammed with way too much information. You could almost hear the dozen or so people who reviewed the letter saying, 'This has to be in there!'"

Editors removed everything that wasn't relevant to the reader. They shortened words and sentences. And the new letter has a friendly tone. It reads like a simple conversation between two people.

Center for Plain Language

In fact, one of the tips Lankarge and Berkenstock encouraged people to try is to picture a real person when writing—a specific person, someone outside the industry, like a neighbor. Then just imagine you're having a conversation with them. You're telling this person some news they need to know. And you're doing it as simply as possible. This approach removes that stiff, artificial barrier between a company and the reader.

That *Before & After* example got plenty of use. It made it into many face-to-face and phone presentations. And it was sent around in e-mail as an introduction to show the value of clear communication.

What part of Aetna implemented the program?

Because Aetna's program started as a truly grassroots effort, it didn't have a single department owner. Or any owner for that matter! People from various departments across the company simply volunteered their time and passion for the subject to keep things afloat and growing.

Later, when things started to get a little more formal, the plain language work landed in the marketing department.

"We had a small team of quality reviewers that followed a content checklist, but we revised and expanded that document with more focus on clear communication and serving the brand," says Melissa Slade, Senior Director, Marketing Communications. "Prior to that, the checklist had been a bit more technical, covering issues like, 'Does this piece have the right disclaimer?'"

 **ACTIONS**

Describe what resources Aetna used or referenced to learn how to develop this program

Because Aetna's Plain Language Initiative started off on the ground, rather than in the halls of the executive suite, there was no kickoff meeting or project plan. The resources the team needed were selected, or created, on the fly.

"When we pitched the idea for plain language to medical directors, nurses, and case managers, we showed videos of real people struggling with health literacy," says Lankarge. "This showed that poor communication can be a patient safety issue."

Anytime an opportunity to advance the cause arose, the team jumped at it, tailoring the message to each audience:

⇒ With medical directors, they talked about poor communication as a patient safety issue.

⇒ With business people, it was about a return on investment.

⇒ With executives, the angle was thought leadership.

⇒ With product owners, it was all about improving the customer experience.

⇒ And with advertising and communications, the talk was about strengthening the brand.

What did it cost Aetna, and was it worth the investment? Are you saving (or did you save) money as a result of doing this? If so, how much?

The small volunteer army accomplished a lot with no funding. A major win was getting the topic of plain language added to the company's yearly Business, Conduct, and Integrity training, a requirement for every employee.

Today, plain language training and a content quality review process are budget items.

"It was worth the investment because we've helped people better understand their health and their benefits and how to use them, and that leads to fewer calls to customer service, which is a huge money-saver," says Lankarge. "Saving money is a great by-product of doing good work, which increases customer satisfaction and patient safety."

 ## PROBLEMS, OBSTACLES, OR CHALLENGES

Discuss the problems, obstacles, or challenges Aetna faced.

Getting the word out about plain language and clear communication started slowly. It was almost a person-to-person approach. But as more and more people became believers, the speed of expansion became like a bad case of the flu.

Berkenstock says, "You'd hear one person on a conference call mention it and then another person would chime in and then another. And I remember being introduced to someone who said, 'Oh, you're the plain language guy.' That's when we knew things were really cooking."

Center for Plain Language

The next challenge was to give people the tools and resources they needed to get the work done and get their managers to buy in to the new approach:

⇒ A quarterly plain language newsletter full of how-to tips

⇒ A monthly feature on the intranet about how to cut business and healthcare jargon

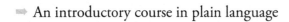

Figure 2. Aetna's quarterly plain language newsletters with information, resources, and tips

⇒ An introductory course in plain language

Once that basic knowledge was established with enough people across the company, the team needed to keep up the interest and momentum. These tactics helped:

⇒ Recognize the good work people do.

⇒ Thank and encourage plain language champions—with an e-mail to the writer and his or her boss.

⇒ Brand a few of the best experts as role models.

⇒ Share examples of challenges and successes.

⇒ Research and test. (This helps everyone get better and prove the value of the work.)

 **PROGRESS**

Does the government or another body regulate your industry?

Healthcare is a regulated industry at both the federal and state levels. Some states dictate what point size the text needs to be. And over the years, more and more states added requirements around reading grade levels. (For example, "Materials must be written at a 5th-grade reading level.")

Center for Plain Language

"We also faced some mandated wording that was not as clear or simple as it could be," Lankarge recalls. "That makes it tricky when we've worked hard to create a clear piece and then find out we have to add language that is different in tone and reading grade level. It's jarring and not a good experience for the reader."

What problems did Aetna focus on first?

The next big step in Aetna's initiative around clear communication was building a process. While a lot of good work was happening across the country, things were not consistent. Writers, reviewers, and others did not have a rule book to follow.

Working on this step started with education. The company needed to recognize that in addition to its main business, it is also, by default, a publisher. Few companies see themselves this way. But starting with that fact helps. Everyone agrees that a publishing company with no proofreaders or without a tight system of quality checks would be a disaster.

This led to the start of Aetna's writer/reviewer training program.

What did the program look like?

Today, Aetna has certified writers and certified quality reviewers. Both groups take a series of classes and have to pass a test.

How many people got involved at beginning?

"We started to advertise the training, mostly on the company intranet," says Lankarge. "Later, after we launched our new brand, we incorporated some of our training into the brand training. We'd make sure people knew that writers had to be certified. And we had different tracks for different types of writing. Marketing is one thing. Writing letters is another."

How does Aetna work with people who don't want change?

The new brand was a major factor in the spread of plain language.

"In the early years, we lost as many battles as we won because there was no higher power to break a tie," says Berkenstock. "A reviewer could just say, 'I like using "physician" better than "doctor,"' and that would be the end of it. But when the new brand came along and we were able to get *Clear Communication* as a key brand element, that changed the game. We didn't have to fight quite as much. Writers could just say, 'This is the Aetna brand,' when they faced someone's opposing personal preference."

To what degree did a fear of "dumbing down" slow progress, and how did Aetna address this?

"Dumbing down" is a phrase often tossed about by people who don't understand clear communication. Some writers or subject matter experts like to show off their deep knowledge by using big words and insider jargon. Others people almost seem embarrassed to be writing in a way they think is beneath them. Many come around once they see that plain language doesn't mean "See Dick run."

"It's always awful to hear that phrase. The best way to combat it is with education. As more and more people joined the clear-communication bandwagon, we were able to just thunder past the 'dumbing down' naysayers," says Lankarge. "For the most part, those old objections are now irrelevant. Most people at Aetna understand why the 'dumbing down' argument doesn't carry any weight."

How did Aetna educate writers to understand technical and complex subject matter and communicate well with technical folks?

In their training for writers and in the quarterly plain language newsletter, Aetna emphasizes the need to work with subject matter experts and to keep asking questions until the writers are confident that they truly understand the material. Only then can the writers translate the message into clear writing that the average person can easily understand. It's hard work. And not everyone can do it well.

How did Aetna engage graphic designers to ensure an easy-to-understand message?

Of course, writing is only one part of clear communication. Design—in print and digital materials—is an equal partner. At Aetna, designers were onboard with clear communication from the start. In fact, they were ahead of the game. They'd been complaining for years about getting too much copy or copy that didn't follow a logical order. Simplicity and order are basic elements that designers need in order to do their jobs well. So they were happy to have more enlightened writers.

How did Aetna keep the program alive over the long term?

Before the launch of the new brand, Aetna had to constantly keep the clear-communication message "in the news." That meant articles, contests, reminders, a celebration for Health Literacy Month, and a host of other actions that were essentially marketing the idea and the ideal they were shooting for.

Center for Plain Language

Now, thanks to clear communication being an official part of the company brand, Aetna feels that plain language is in its DNA. That doesn't mean things are perfect; it's always a work in progress. But a strong foundation had been established.

Was there an enforcement component?

Enforcing the new principles grew as clear communication became part of the brand and as the quality review process was expanded. Plain language and clear communication are always part of the conversation now.

Does Aetna reward those who do a great job using plain language?

Early on in the program's growth, recognizing and rewarding people for their support and good work was crucial to the program's success. One year the team highlighted a different plain language champion each month and then awarded one of them Plain Language Champion of the Year.

People could also send Good Job certificates to writers and designers (and their managers) to say "congrats" for an exceptional piece of work.

There were also rewrite contests with awards like gift certificates and a drawing for an iPod. (Yes, that's how long ago the program started; iPods were a hot item.)

One of the best rewards is to be invited to join the Aetna table at the annual ClearMark Awards in Washington DC, to see all the entries and meet folks with a similar passion for plain language.

 **OUTCOMES**

Did Aetna meet its initial goals? If so, how did you know?

The initial goal was clear: education and awareness. "We knew things were changing for the better when we'd get slammed with e-mail requests to do a plain language review," says Lankarge.

There was one very hectic year, when Lankarge and Berkenstock tried to review anything that anyone in the company sent to them. This wasn't sustainable, of course. But that's when upper-level management began to see the need for something formal. One executive said, "We need to institutionalize what you two are doing off the sides of your desks."

Was your program a success, and how did you measure this?

Two big wins helped the program grow and flourish.

Seeing clear communication added to the brand was phenomenal. The writers, editors, and designers who had pushed this effort for so long were walking around as if they had helium in their chests. They had a lot to be proud of.

Writers and communicators don't always get to make a difference in the lives of real people, like nurses, case managers, and health coaches do. But with this change—making the language easier to understand—the communicators at Aetna are making life better for many people.

The first win…

Every Aetna employee, every year, takes a "business conduct and integrity" course. It's an online tutorial about the company's values and rules. A section was added to that yearly training about plain language and clear communication. Every employee was made aware of how important this was to the company.

The second win…

A few years later, Aetna updated its brand with a new logo, a new look and a new voice. Communicating clearly was a key part of the new voice. It stated "We write and speak in simple, direct language that's easy to understand." And the brand guidebook included examples.

And it's good to remember that clear communication isn't just for people who have poor reading skills. Nor is it just for people who are less educated. It's for people who are sick, for one thing. And they shouldn't have to wade through healthcare mumbo-jumbo. They want to get through the system and back to their lives.

Lots of research shows that busy, smart, and educated people prefer simplicity and clarity, too. But something strange can happen to many people when they walk into work in the morning. They forget they are regular people, like consumers and shoppers. And they fail to see things from an outside perspective. Aetna's focus on clear communication helps to balance that out.

How many people are involved now (as opposed to at the start)?

When plain language and clear communication started at Aetna, it was in the hands of a small group of dedicated volunteers. That group grew to include others who shared the same thoughts around clear communication but who hadn't connected with people around the company who wanted to accomplish similar goals.

Center for Plain Language

For a number of years, this amorphous group—a very active core, with another group offering support—kept things alive. Today, the number of people involved is in the hundreds. This includes all those who have gone through the training and who review the material as well as the internal teams who need material created and who have to understand the goals and voice of the new brand.

What positive comments did Aetna receive from your staff or from customers?

Each year, one department in the company tests the same handful of materials they produce for Open Enrollment, the period when people choose their health plans for the year. Flyers and brochures about plans and products are tested with real customers.

People give feedback on the general impression of the materials, and on the specific pictures, headlines, body copy, and call-and to-action text. That feedback is then used to revise the pieces for the next year.

If a high percentage of reviewers say, "I love how you explained copays," that same definition can be used in other pieces. And when people say, "Why do you keep assuming I know what coinsurance is?" the team knows they need to do a better job explaining that concept.

Any negative reaction?

Despite the progress, the clear communication practitioners and evangelists still, on occasion, run into someone who says, "Oh, you want me to dumb it down."

Lankarge says she takes a deep breath and replies like this…

"The only dumb thing is to keep giving people complicated information they can't use. Our job is not to cram every detail about healthcare and insurance into our materials. The average person doesn't need that. When I take my car to the service station, I don't need my mechanic to go into the details of how my catalytic converter works and why it failed. I just need to know he's going to fix it and how much it will cost."

Does plain language feel like part of your Aetna's culture or are you still working on that?

The team knew their work was becoming real when people on conference calls would say, "Did you run this by the plain language folks?" Instead of it being a "nice-to-have," it became the standard.

What do you wish Aetna had done differently?

The process to incorporate clear communication into daily life at Aetna was long and slow.

 Center for Plain Language

"I wish we could have gone faster," says Lankarge. "I wish we could have gotten support and money sooner."

On the positive side, that slow growth, which started with the belief and passion of frontline communicators (writers, editors, designers) meant that clear communication had an organic birth. As its acceptance grew and spread, people had time to take it in and make it their own. There was a certain pride in the fact that the experts started this and got the company to recognize and support it.

What are Aetna's goals/plans for the future?

Now the goal is to make sure this work stays front and center. Aetna is becoming a more consumer-facing company. They were business-to-business for most of its existence, selling health plan packages to employers. But the world of healthcare has changed dramatically. The consumer is "king" now. And consumers are less forgiving when things are unclear or confusing, especially now that they are paying for more of their healthcare. Aetna's goal is to create an experience that mirrors the experiences people have with other top brands, from Amazon to Zappos.

What advice would you give an organization looking to start its own program?

One surprising thing that the Aetna team learned when they started all this work was that people were looking for experts to make decisions. People were not opposed to being told, "This is the rule." In fact, it made their lives easier. They no longer had to argue about making communications materials clearer or simpler. They could just say, "This is our brand, and we follow and support it."

So the advice from Lankarge and others at Aetna who helped create a culture of clear communication is this: "If no one in your organization is making these decisions, you should do it. Proceed until apprehended!"

You can become the expert who pushes the effort forward. Don't wait for someone else or someone higher up the chain to do it. Find like-minded people in your company or organization, and band together.

Convert coworkers through education. Appeal to their common sense and desire for success. You may have to build relationships one at a time. Is it slow going? Yes. But each person you bring into the fold becomes a supporter—or even better—an evangelist. You'll never convince everyone. But you'll eventually tip the balance in favor of clear communication. And there is no downside to that.

The Minnesota Department of Revenue (Revenue) manages the state's revenue system and administers state tax laws. In all, it manages more than thirty different taxes and collects more than $20.5 billion annually.

This money funds education, local government aid, property tax relief, social service programs, highways, economic development incentives, and grants for businesses and other state programs and operations.

An interview with...

Melissa Donndelinger, MPM, PMP
Editorial Coordinator at the Minnesota Department
of Revenue

www.revenue.state.mn.us

IDENTIFIABLE PROBLEM

What prompted Revenue to start a plain language program?

The Minnesota Department of Revenue (Revenue) needed to combine tax enforcement with taxpayer education and outreach. This meant seeing things from the customer's point of view and making sure customer communication was as clear as possible.

The challenge, of course, is that the communications need to be understandable and meet the needs of the law. Plain language was an ideal tool to drive this customer service approach.

"As an agency," says Editorial Coordinator Melissa Donndelinger, "we're always looking for ways to become more efficient and provide better customer service."

SPECIFIC GOALS

What were Revenue's goals at the start?

The original objectives were modest: to develop a process and to ensure that plain language standards could be used in all stakeholder communication.

As a first step, Revenue knew that it had to improve awareness for plain language writing, editing, and approval with its own employees. It then looked at what areas of communication would benefit from a plain language review. Finally, it developed standards for plain language communication and made sure that these standards were communicated across the department.

As the project evolved, the department added goals around writing, editing, and approving plain language content.

ACTIONS

What problems did Revenue focus on first?

Training was a key part of the approach. After the project manager and editing staff met with each division about their editorial needs, Revenue hired a consultant to train its staff.

Center for Plain Language

Training was mandatory for management and division-identified members. Initially, 316 employees (out of approximately 1,500) were trained by the consultant, and Revenue has since trained many others.

"Managers were required to attend a half-day training session," reported Donndelinger, "and division members, an in-depth and hands-on two-day training session. We filled additional slots with our website contributors, trainers, and people from the procedures and outreach teams."

[316 out of roughly 1,500 employees: trained!]

Trainers in the Employee Development Services unit also started incorporating the consultant's methodology and approach into existing materials to create a repeatable internal training session.

What part of Revenue implemented the program, and what did the program look like?

The project manager and project sponsor, both from the Communications Division, aimed to make this a department-wide project. There was also a lot of support from the executive leadership of the agency.

Here's what Revenue did:

Step #1: Identified two to three people in each division to join an in-depth, two-day training session. They became the Division Plain Language Champions.

Step #2: Developed a procedure for when and how to request a review from the legal division.

"Shortly after training," says Donndelinger, "we changed the project scope to include a pilot cluster of content to test the process we were developing."

Step #3: Rewrote two letters using plain language and conducted usability testing on a handful of documents and webpages that we had put into plain language.

Step #4: Made changes to the process and materials based on the pilot project and usability testing.

Center for Plain Language

Step #5: After multiple clusters and changes to the review schedule and process, closed the project formally.

Step #6: Rolled out Plain Language 2.0 that empowered the divisions to take more editorial ownership of their materials.

How many people got involved at the beginning?

Steering Team	Executive Sponsor
	Project Owner
	Project Manager
	Editor-in-Chief (Project Lead)
	Communications GenTax Coordinator* *GenTax® is an integrated tax management system.
Project Team	Project Manager
	Project Lead
	Communications GenTax Coordinator
	Technical Expert (for letters development)
Trainers	Consultant
	Agency trainers in the Employee Development Services unit

How did Revenue engage graphic designers (and others) to ensure an easy-to-understand message?

As members of the Communications Division, all graphic designers attended the plain language training. In this way, the practices and plain language habits became everyday tactics that they naturally incorporated into graphic design.

Revenue also involved the legal team right away, by developing a process that included when and how to request a legal review.

Center for Plain Language

"Legal review is essential for Revenue," says Donndelinger, "because communication needs to be easy to understand and accurate in terms of Minnesota law."

What did it cost Revenue and was it worth the investment? Are you saving (or did you save) money as a result of doing this? If so, how much?

300 training and consulting hours (18 months)

=

$75,000

"The funding was worth the investment," explains Donndelinger, "because the consultant set a tone and high standards for our initiative. The consultant helped to create buy-in in the department."

A further cost consideration was employee time. Because plain language was important to enhancing the work that the agency does with customers, the investment was considered well worth it.

How many people are involved now (as opposed to at the start)?

The program is now managed by one person in the Communications Division. This person works closely with the division and the Communications GenTax Coordinator. On top of that, Revenue now boasts about thirty Plain Language Champions who focus on the work in each division.

"All Revenue employees are involved with plain language to some degree," says Donndelinger, "whether they are writing, editing, or using the material—they are a part of the process and culture."

Does Revenue reward those who do a great job using plain language?

Revenue makes sure to communicate big and little wins.

Center for Plain Language

Celebration!

To celebrate the end of the official project, Revenue held a recognition event for the Steering Team, Project Team, and Division Plain Language Champions and handed out certificates.

Badges

Individual rewards are also key to keeping the momentum going. Revenue created paper badges to be handed out—with room for a personal message on the back— when someone is noticed for using plain language.

PROBLEMS, OBSTACLES, OR CHALLENGES

What were the barriers for starting the program?

As with any change in a large organization, the transition to using this way of communicating with customers took time and effort. The main barriers were:

⇒ Creating buy-in that plain language techniques did not "dumb down" materials or make them legally inaccurate.

⇒ Needing plain language expertise.

⇒ Committing staff time and resources to participate in training, develop processes, and write and edit in plain language.

PROGRESS

How does Revenue work with people who don't want change? What advice would you give others who are facing this challenge?

When asked about her lessons learned, Donndelinger offered up the following list:

⇒ Use customer experience to reinforce the need to change and to show the value of using plain language.

⇒ Address the root cause of why people may be hesitant to adapt to the new practices.

⇒ Offer resources in many methodologies to address any concerns employees may have and that may contribute to their hesitations.

Center for Plain Language

→ Have patience.

→ Use comments (in Microsoft Word) to explain changes and to help writers understand the reason for the changes.

→ Get full management support. They must invest in the time and resources to do the program right.

→ Have a fluid process: allow for changes and a loose timeline to improve your materials so that they work for your customers—both internally and externally.

→ Empower staff to take ownership of the quality of the materials sent from the organization.

→ Conduct usability testing, and let your writers observe some of the testing sessions so they can see firsthand how customers are responding to materials.

→ Foster open, honest, and frequent communication with the entire organization— including processes, tactics, rationales, and successes.

→ Keep communication, marketing, and resources current and relevant.

To what degree did a fear of "dumbing down" slow progress, and how did you address this?

"The fear [of dumbing down] definitely existed and, to some degree, there is still some concern," admits Donndelinger.

That said, Revenue has made great progress and is continually educating and communicating with people on industry best standards, usability results, and rationale for using simpler words and phrases. This takes time and patience.

For example, Revenue took the time at the beginning to explain the "why" of edits, to make sure people understood the changes and stayed on board with the project. It also asked employees to focus on content from the customer's perspective.

How did Revenue educate writers to understand technical and complex subject matter and communicate well with technical folks?

The project team met regularly about business design, formatting, and processing for letters. These discussions were often related to what technical capabilities were available.

For technical and complex content, Revenue encouraged and challenged writers to look from the customer's perspective—provide context and use everyday words and phrases.

"Conducting usability testing after the pilot cluster allowed us to use customer interactions and feedback to justify further actions and rationales," says Donndelinger.

Center for Plain Language

 **OUTCOMES**

Did Revenue meet its initial goals? If so, how did it know?

["Yes, we did!"]

Revenue considers its project a major success for a number of reasons:

First, plain language has largely become part of its culture—a huge success for any project—but even more so for a large organization where changing culture is a long process.

Second, Revenue now boasts a sustainable plain language process and editorial standards that are customer focused. This means that training is always available to employees, writing tips are widely shared, and plain language methodology and practices are part of all planning discussions.

Third, Revenue received many positive news clippings and social media posts regarding "crisp" and "clearly stated" messaging and information.

Fourth, every time Revenue posts a writing tip or announcement about a change or success, it always receives at least one anecdotal e-mail from an employee conveying thanks or acknowledging the impact of the tip or effort.

Fifth, usability testers are often quoted as saying, "Thank you for doing this!"

Did Revenue meet additional goals?

"Shortly after training," says Donndelinger, "we changed the project scope to include a pilot cluster of content to test the process we were developing."

But Revenue had other successes, too.

For example, to help employees consult and implement plain language guidelines, it converted the style guide from a PDF document to an electronic format, where each entry had its own page. It also created a *Formatting Letters Guidelines* document for technical staff.

Center for Plain Language

The State of Plain Language

Four out of five people chose direct deposit for refunds last filing season

98% reduction in number of renters trying to free file property tax refunds electronically as homeowners

One agency footer, reduced from 60 agency footers before plain language

2,100 views of the agency Style Guide in 8 months

2,348 views of the plain language video through Sept. 30

Received 2014 State Government Innovation Award

Say It Simply
Plain Language

MINNESOTA · REVENUE

Figure 3. Say It Simply announcement of plain language success

Awareness was always a key pillar of this project, so Revenue devoted resources to branding plain language as Say It Simply and created an intranet site with targeted resources and information.

In addition, it created four plain language marketing videos. In fact, one video was modified for public use and is now available on Governor Mark Dayton's YouTube channel.

The final triumph was that the project transitioned into a program, which is managed by the Communications Division.

Center for Plain Language

Was Revenue's program a success, and how was this measured?

Revenue's initiative sparked Governor Dayton to sign an executive order implementing plain language in the executive branch. Revenue is seen as a state leader and advisor.	**2014** Revenue received the 2014 State Government Innovation Award and 2014 Governor's Continuous Improvement Award.
Revenue was also a featured storyteller at the Minnesota Social Impact Center's launch event.	**12** Revenue has consulted with almost a dozen other states and three state agencies about plain language best practices and lessons learned.
Usability testing results comparing before and after versions show an increase in customer satisfaction and ease of understanding and a decrease in time on task.	**65%** Revenue collaborated and streamlined its call messages, resulting in a 65% reduction in the number of messages.
98% Revenue revamped web content about property tax refunds with a customer focus, resulting in a 98% decrease in renters who mistakenly file as homeowners through our website.	**1,000%** Revenue has facilitated plain language training to over 1,000 people outside of Revenue, including Governor's Office staff, state employees in other state agencies, and property tax assessors—it also is continually being asked to present.

What does Revenue wish it had done differently?

"It would be nice to have tangible metrics," suggests Donndelinger, "related to response time—through phone, e-mail, or mail—or follow-up action."

Center for Plain Language

She went on to say that because so much of plain language is qualitatively measured, it is difficult to say whether a single customer letter resulted in an increase or decrease of something. There are simply too many outside factors. However, customers have said communications from Revenue are clearer than those from some other organizations that they interact with.

What are Revenue's goals/plans for the future?

Revenue is not done yet. It will now focus on providing more resources and attention to the Division Plain Language Champions to empower them to be the experts for each division's plain language work. Revenue will also conduct another round of usability testing to confirm that they are still meeting the needs of customers and identifying ways to continue to improve.

Center for Plain Language

The United States Fish and Wildlife Service (Service) is a bureau within the Department of the Interior. This bureau manages the 150-million-acre National Wildlife Refuge System, which consists of more than 560 national wildlife refuges and thousands of small wetlands and other special management areas. Under the fisheries program the Service also operates 70 national fish hatcheries, 65 fishery resource offices, and 86 ecological services field stations.

Service programs are among the oldest in the world dedicated to natural resource conservation: the history of the Service can be traced back to 1871. As a decentralized organization (headquarters in Washington DC, and regional and field offices dispersed throughout the nation), the Service employs approximately 9,000 people.

An interview with...

Krista Bibb
USFWS Writer and Editor

www.fws.gov

Center for Plain Language

IDENTIFIABLE PROBLEM

What prompted the Service to start a plain language program?

"There is no formal plain language program at the U.S. Fish and Wildlife Service (Service)," according to Krista Bibb, a Service writer and editor. The interest in plain language started prior to the 2010 Plain Writing Act (Act), stemming from a few individuals with an interest in making the content of Service products easier to understand.

SPECIFIC GOALS

What were the Service's goals at the start?

Bibb says, "The goals, at the start, were to make Service policies easier to understand."

This continues to be the main focus, even though it is often difficult with so many types of Service-related documents that have different audiences and serve different purposes. Regulations, Service Manual chapters, and other official policies are routed through the Service's Division of Policy, Performance, and Management Programs (PPM). This gives PPM the opportunity to review and make changes that reflect clear language principles. However, there are other types of documents (for example, permits) that do not go through this chain of approval.

"Unless there is a champion working in these areas, there is no one monitoring for plain language," says Bibb.

Does the government or another body regulate your industry?

The Service must abide by all laws and regulations that instruct federal agencies on how to correspond clearly with the public.

Center for Plain Language

ACTIONS

What part of the Service was responsible for implementing a plain language program?

The staff at PPM and other staff started emphasizing plain language prior to the Act. The initiative continues through the work of PPM and other champions who encourage plain language and clear communication in their respective programs.

PPM implements the program by encouraging others to attend trainings and to make corrections themselves. By making corrections themselves, some use this as a learning experience and improve. Others just create what first comes to mind and then leave the rest of the heavy lifting to PPM.

PPM supports a plain language webpage (http://www.fws.gov/pdm/plainlang.html) to help those who are interested.

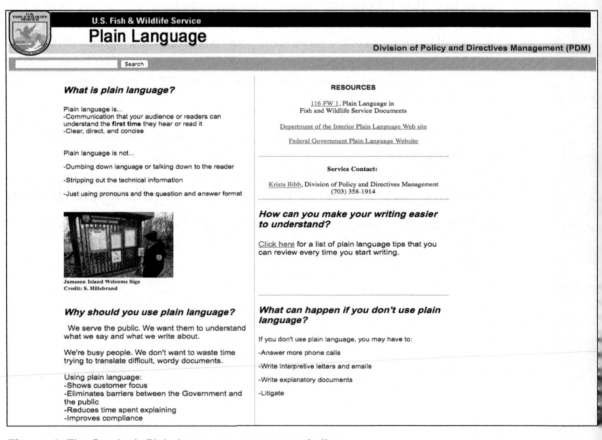

Figure 4. The Service's Plain Language resource website

Center for Plain Language

PROBLEMS, OBSTACLES, OR CHALLENGES

What are some of the barriers the Service faces in getting a program started?

Bibb noted a few of the barriers to starting a program at the Service:

- ⇒ Lack of dedicated funds
- ⇒ No designated staff
- ⇒ Long-term government employees who do not see the value
- ⇒ Other priorities

"There are many people working in government that have a perspective that if a document isn't written in bureaucratic, 'governmenty' language, then it isn't correct," comments Bibb.

What problems are you focusing on first?

"A plain language initiative is not supported from the top down as a priority," says Bibb, "so the focus of PPM is to make corrections, encourage training, try to get staff to embrace plain language as much as possible, and hope for support from Service staff."

The strategy is to start by building rapport and trust. PPM is trying to make staff accountable for their language choices and is focused on encouraging active voice. "It is amazing how many people do not understand what active voice is," comments Bibb.

Another strategy is to strive for internal consistency, which varies by the person and the learning they adopt. The Service offers some online courses through the National Conservation Training Center (NCTC). Contracting with Michelle Baker's Communication (http://conservationwritingpro.com) is a key program at the moment, until plain language becomes a priority for the Service.

PROGRESS

What does the program look like, and how many people are involved?

The program isn't anything formal or official. It started with two people, then quickly increased to four. And a handful of people continue to lend support Service-wide.

Center for Plain Language

How does the Service work with people who don't want change?

"Our initial approach is to try to show them the benefits of clear writing," states Bibb. "If we can make the connection that less confusion leads to less need to respond to unclear direction, it becomes easier in the long run.

"Doing the work for them often comes into play," notes Bibb. "People have to accept clear writing as a priority. Minimizing its importance reduces their desire to spend time and energy 'polishing' their work."

To what degree did a fear of "dumbing down" slow progress, and how did the Service address this?

This has not been an issue. The Service has been more concerned about those who insist on the content sounding legal.

How did the Service educate writers to understand technical and complex subject matter and communicate well with technical folks?

"Frankly," states Bibb, "we edit for them."

The Service hopes to lead by example, but this approach has its limits. A good plain language communicator is not always a subject matter expert (SME). So we need to engage SMEs; otherwise the message to the public may be not only unclear but also incorrect.

How has the Service kept the program alive over the long term?

At this point, there is no guarantee of longevity. Once the interested people leave, the initiative might go with them.

 **OUTCOMES**

Was the Service's program a success, and how did you measure this?

"A program is evolving," says Bibb, "and we do see some successes, but it is mostly anecdotal."

Center for Plain Language

What positive comments did the Service get from its staff or from customers?

Some of the feedback indicates that the documents using clear writing are more professional. Various programs, with staff embracing plain language proactively, have had good feedback from the public regarding easier-to-understand regulations.

Any negative reaction?

Some people, mostly staff, want to know: "Why are you doing this?"

What did it cost the Service, and has it been worth the investment?

The Service has not received any budget or funding for a plain language program. However, the few staff members who are pro-plain-language have invested their time and energy into making the Service content simpler and clearer.

How many people are involved now (as opposed to at the start)?

Currently, there are five people in PPM promoting plain language. Plus, there is a handful of supporters.

Does plain language feel like part of the Service's culture, or are you still working on that?

Definitely still working on it! The Service did get good marks last year, despite having only a handful of plain language advocates.

What advice would you give an organization looking to start its own program?

There are three key points that are important when trying to start a plain language program:

- Get management support!
- Dedicate resources.
- Provide incentives.

Center for Plain Language

Deloitte New Zealand is the New Zealand member firm of Deloitte Touche Tohmatsu Limited, a global professional services firm with a network of member firms in more than 150 countries, Deloitte brings world-class capabilities and high-quality service to clients, delivering the insights they need to address their most complex business challenges.

Deloitte New Zealand employs over 1,000 professionals and provides audit, tax, technology and systems, strategy, performance improvement, risk management, corporate finance, business recovery, forensics, and accounting services.

An interview with...

Matt Huntington
Senior Communications Manager, Deloitte NZ

Deloitte.

www.deloitte.com

IDENTIFIABLE PROBLEM

What prompted Deloitte New Zealand to start a plain language program?

Deloitte gauges its performance in part by a national Market Perception Survey that ranks similar consulting firms. Though "Talk straight" is one of Deloitte's corporate values, the company received low scores in "quality communications," namely clarity and communication, in the 2013 survey. But Deloitte was not alone in this. Its competitors also struggled in this area.

In 2014, Deloitte decided it was time to do something about this issue. Senior Communications Manager Matt Huntington and a small team reviewed the company's communications. They determined that their low scores were the result of non-reader-focused writing across all types of consulting.

Huntington explains, "Starting a plain language program was more than a good practice. It was also a way to get a leg up on the competition."

SPECIFIC GOALS

What were Deloitte's initial goals?

Huntington's initial proposal to the company's partner group included three goals of the Plain English campaign:

- Get all Deloitte people writing in plain English.
- Address weaknesses identified in the 2013 Market Perceptions around "quality communications."
- Raise the bar overall on written communication at Deloitte.

He hoped to reach these goals by achieving five objectives:

- Create awareness of the importance of plain English.
- Demonstrate effective written communication.
- Provide plain English resources.
- Embed plain English into the Deloitte culture.
- Win a 2014 WriteMark Plain English Award.

 Center for Plain Language

The plan would include five phases: tease, build awareness, inspire and educate, engage, and follow up and celebrate. There were no client-specific goals. Rather, Huntington and his team believed that achievement of their company goals would indicate overall improvement for clients.

Matt describes the company's "mood" as competitive. Winning the WriteMark award was a good incentive for the plain language initiative team, CEO, and other company executives. Competing against other regional locations and service lines proved to be a big enough incentive for most employees.

 **ACTIONS**

How many people got involved at the beginning?

The initial plain language team included Huntington and several other employees. Hunting explained that the team's first job was to "sell" the idea to Chief Executive Officer Thomas Pippos and other high-level executives. Huntington emphasized the importance of spending time getting support at this level. Pippos was enthusiastic about this campaign, and his enthusiasm spread to executives throughout the company. Thanks to their approval, Matt and his team had access to all the resources they needed to develop a comprehensive plan.

What part of Deloitte's organization implemented the program?

The plain English team was largely people in communications and design, but it also included other service lines and professionals, including IT.

What were the barriers for starting the program?

The team felt people would not participate or give plain English training enough attention if it was delivered in lessons or other methods that "felt like English class." This is why all elements of their program infused humor and focused on competitive games using plain language as the content.

To further encourage participation, the team framed the campaign as a competition. Games and quizzes pitted location against location and department against department, and the key to success was mastery of plain English.

What problems did Deloitte focus on first?

Huntington and his team analyzed various written documents for specific areas of weakness. They pinpointed four types of errors: wordiness, jargon, complex technological writing, and old-fashioned/dated language.

Center for Plain Language

What did the program look like?

After gaining top-down support, the plain English team created a five-phase action plan. Participation was optional. The team offered incentives in the form of competitions and prizes and aimed for a participation rate of 40 percent.

Phase One – Tease

Goal: Generate interest in the campaign, and "get people talking."

Length: One week

This phase was intentionally vague. From the four previously identified types of errors, the team created archetypal characters. Wordiness became "the rambler," who uses twenty words when ten will do. Jargon became "the jargon master," who uses language unlikely to be understood by someone outside of that field. Complex technological writing became "the technocrat," who uses overly technical language. And old-fashioned/dated language became "the ye olde," who uses outdated words, phrases, or syntax. The team created Wanted posters for each character. All were "wanted for crimes against the English language." They displayed the posters in highly trafficked areas of every Deloitte location.

Figure 5. Sample Wanted poster to "get people talking"

Center for Plain Language

Phase Two – Build Awareness

Goal: Introduce plain English and its benefits.

Length: One week

For this phase, the team created a new section of the company's intranet. There, employees could find a variety of resources and links about plain English and an upcoming, companywide competition. Resources included explanations and examples of plain English as well as basic rules:

- Use active voice.
- Keep to one idea per sentence.
- Make professional writing a habit.
- Explain acronyms and abbreviations.
- Use simple, everyday words.
- Avoid redundant words.
- Minimize the use of jargon.
- Check capitalization and punctuation.

To kick things off, employees received a link to a video starring an executive dressed as a Wild West sheriff. A voiceover announces, "We're looking for a few plain English gunslingers to help clean up this town."

Phase Three – Inspire and Educate

Goal: Show how everyone can make a difference using plain English.

Length: One week

Continuing to develop people's plain English skills, the team published three intranet homepage stories in Q&A format. Whenever Deloitte gains a new partner, its introduction materials include a Q&A story on the intranet, so the team chose this style for its effectiveness and familiarity. These stories included the archetypal characters and "over-the-top language that each archetype tends toward" as well as their typical errors. Links to plain English resources let employees delve deeper and learn more.

Center for Plain Language

Phase Four – Engage

Goal: Put plain English into practice.

Length: Two weeks

This phase encouraged employees to interact with the material and improve their skills. Campaign literature explains that Huntington and his team "knew from past internal campaigns that Deloitte people are very competitive—between our internal service lines and between our regional offices. So (the team) created two online plain English quizzes, released over two weeks, to engage staff with the topic of plain English and to test their understanding of it." They made quizzes less like traditional school tests by using humor and visually engaging graphics. Popular Buzzfeed and other social media quizzes served as models. They also used online learning development software (for example, Adobe Captivate) to build the quizzes. Employees had access to each 13-question quiz for one week.

Each week began with an invitation from the CEO via e-mail and the intranet homepage to take the quiz. Service line leaders also urged their staff to take the quiz to help the region and service line "achieve 'plain English glory.'"

The quizzes aligned with the now-familiar archetypal characters. Software tracked quiz results, revealing each person's writing "character." The team wrote and sent one of five form e-mails— one for each archetype and one for someone with perfect results, with resources specific to the quiz-taker's character.

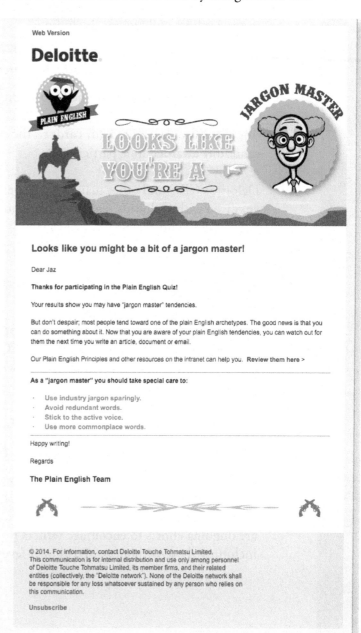

Figure 6. Sample e-mail sent to plain English quiz-takers

Center for Plain Language

The team also tracked quiz results and posted a scoreboard showing different regions' and service lines' progress on their intranets, to keep staff motivated.

Phase 5 – Follow Up and Celebrate

Goal: Keep up momentum, and make plain English part of Deloitte culture.

Length: Ongoing

Huntington and his team sent personalized e-mails to all participants. They posted final scores and announced individual winners. Four team prizes and trophies were awarded to service lines and regions, including:

- ⇒ Highest combined participation rate on both quizzes.
- ⇒ Highest average combined scores on both quizzes.

The team also distributed gift cards to the two highest scoring individuals and two randomly awarded quiz participants.

Deloitte's CEO and other management personnel presented the trophies, which were engraved with Deloitte's plain English logo. They also distributed branded gift baskets and boxes of chocolates.

 ## PROBLEMS, OBSTACLES, OR CHALLENGES

Huntington attributes the lack of major problems, obstacles, or challenges to spending a lot of time getting support from the CEO and other top executives. That support enabled them to assemble a strong team with the time and resources necessary for a project of this size.

To what degree did a fear of "dumbing down" slow progress, and how did Deloitte address this?

Huntington explained that it was and remains challenging to convince technological and legal departments that plain language does not mean "dumbing down" their writing. Technological writing can be too complex, and legal writing is rife with jargon. There are ongoing efforts to encourage writers in all departments to write to their audiences, including those without a professional-level familiarity with the topic.

Center for Plain Language

PROGRESS

How many people are involved now (as opposed to at the start)?

The plain English team had high hopes for participation, aiming for 40 percent. In the end, up to 45% of employees participated in the quizzes and accessed plain English resources.

OUTCOMES

Were the organization's goals met?

Although Huntington feels it will take more work to get "all Deloitte people writing in plain English," they did address weaknesses identified in the 2013 Market Perceptions Survey around "quality communications," and they did raise the bar overall on written communications.

The team reached all five of their objectives.

Objective 1: Create awareness of the importance of plain English.

- **45.2% of staff took one of the plain English quizzes.**

- **The average score across both quizzes was 71.**

- **38% of those who took the quiz had "technocrat" tendencies.**

- **26% of those who took the quiz had "rambler" tendencies.**

- **21% of those who took the quiz had "jargon master" tendencies.**

- **13% of those who took the quiz had "ye olde" tendencies.**

- **2% of those who took the quiz achieved perfect scores.**

Objective 2: Demonstrate effective written communication.

- **853 views of the plain English homepage**
  (Note: Deloitte has 1000 employees.)

- **733 views of the plain English principles page**

- **676 views of the plain English process page**

- **1,621 views of the quiz scoreboard page**

Objective 3: Provide plain English resources.

- **Posters, e-mails, intranet resources and stories, quizzes, printed materials**

Objective 4: Embed plain English into the Deloitte culture.

- **Plain English training is now a part of new-employee training.**

- **Employees continue to submit examples of good plain English and bad writing to the team, who adds the examples to the intranet resource pages.**

- **People warn each other not to be a "rambler" or a "jargon master."**

Objective 5: Win a 2014 WriteMark Plain English Award.

- **In 2014, Deloitte won the *Plain English Champion – Best Organisation* award, the highest of the WriteMark Plain English Awards.**

 Center for Plain Language

What positive comments did Deloitte get from its staff or from customers?

Huntington's team has received positive feedback from employees and company leaders. Deloitte's management group was positive and found that the campaign did a good job supporting the company's pursuit of better documentation and client communication.

What did this campaign cost the organization?

There was a modest budget for the campaign covering the costs of the Adobe Captivate software license, trophies, gift baskets, and gift cards. All the design, printing, etc., was done in-house. The largest cost was around the resourcing required to develop and implement the campaign. Both the team and the company feel that the campaign was well worth the investment in time and money.

Does plain language feel like part of Deloitte's culture, or are you still working on that?

Huntington and his team would like to see continued improvements and a stronger plain language culture. Plain language instruction is now part of new-employee training. Huntington feels it would be pragmatic to include it in partner training, as employees tend to match their supervisors' writing styles. He also sees value in approaching plain English from an editing perspective. He would like to see people simplify and clarify their writing during the editing process instead of aiming for a perfect, plain English first draft.

What are your goals/plans for the future?

Huntington says, "We will refresh" people's plain English awareness and skills. His team hopes to release updated games and quizzes in 2016/2017.

What do you wish you had done differently?

"We could have built on the momentum of the campaign and the award," Huntington says. "I would pay more attention to follow-up."

What advice would you give an organization looking to start its own program?

⇒ Get backing from top execs first. Spend time garnering the support of the CEO and other high-level executives.

⇒ Pay attention to the follow-up phase to keep up the momentum. Go in knowing how you are going to do this.

⇒ Have fun.

⇒ Consider competition.

Center for Plain Language

Healthwise is a global provider of health information, decision support tools, behavior change assistance, and personal care planning for the top health plans, care management companies, hospitals, and consumer health portals. Each year, millions of people use Healthwise content and tools to manage their health, make better health decisions, and live healthier lives.

Founded in 1975, Healthwise is a nonprofit organization dedicated to helping people make better health decisions, and to putting all of our resources into solutions that help us achieve that mission. The organization's expertise lies in creating health content and decision support tools that are easy to understand, engaging, and motivating—and that fit into the delivery of care.

An interview with...

Karen Baker, MHS
Vice President of Mission Initiatives

She sets the pace and direction for plain language and health literacy, leveraging communications expertise and commitment to editorial excellence.

www.healthwise.org

IDENTIFIABLE PROBLEM

What prompted Healthwise to start a plain language program?

In 1975, when Don Kemper founded Healthwise, the nonprofit's mission was to help people make better health decisions. The company's goal has always been to give people evidence-based health information that they can understand and use.

You might even say plain language has been in the bloodstream of Healthwise from day one.

"People can't engage in their care, take care of themselves, or decide what treatment to have or not have unless they know and understand the facts, their options, and the risks and benefits," says Karen Baker, Vice President of Mission Initiatives.

"There wasn't one designated day when we launched a plain language program. It evolved from our roots, from our mission. Way back in 1997, Healthwise had its first plain language training. By 2005, plain language was in the strategic plan. Today, it's embedded in our culture and our brand."

SPECIFIC GOALS

What were Healthwise's goals at the start?

Although Healthwise is a nonprofit with a worthy mission to help people, it is also a business, licensing products that consumers can use and that doctors, coaches, and care managers can prescribe. None of those people would use or recommend Healthwise content if it didn't meet their needs. Plain language is a tool to ensure clear communication in healthcare, a place where so much communication is far from clear.

What part of the Healthwise organization implemented the program?

The Healthwise program started at the top, with founder and CEO, Don Kemper, who was heard to say: "Medical gobbledygook robs people of their autonomy. Without understanding, they have no real say in their care. Plain language gives them back their say."

Center for Plain Language

The Content Team does much of the day-to-day work to create and transform content, along with the Medical Team, which reviews everything for accuracy. Visual and interactive content experts also contribute. There are user researchers/testers. And out in the field, sales and other market-facing teams explain to prospects and clients what the company is doing with clear communication and why.

 **ACTIONS**

What did the program look like?

As the program grew, more elements were added to the basic training:

⇒ Guidelines, style guides, and checklists—and ongoing training

⇒ Content planning

⇒ Editorial support

⇒ Conversations at all-staff meetings

⇒ Calling out colleagues for not using plain language (in a good-natured way!)

⇒ Building plain language into performance appraisals and the strategic plan

⇒ Distributing a Plain Language Bulletin with tips and glossary examples

⇒ Celebrating Grammar Day with contests and prizes

⇒ Sharing plain M&Ms on International Plain Language Day

Figure 7. Plain M&Ms shared annually on International Plain Language Day

How many people got involved at the beginning?

The entire company (about 270 people) is involved in the work to simplify the often-complex world of diseases and conditions. "We wouldn't have succeeded if we didn't engage the entire organization," says Baker.

How does Healthwise work with people (at various levels of authority) who don't want change?

Way back, around the time of the company's first training, someone made this now-infamous comment: "Not everyone may be able to read our product, and that's okay."

But it wasn't.

The mission made things clear: To help people (and that's *all* people) make better health decisions.

Some people who resist change just need help understanding why things are changing. Explaining this wasn't hard for Healthwise to do, given its mission.

Other people simply needed a different level or kind of training. The company made sure people got that—and it still provides training today.

 ## PROBLEMS, OBSTACLES, OR CHALLENGES

Discuss the problems, obstacles, or challenges that Healthwise faced.

Healthwise's biggest challenge lie in its thousands of pages of content that was patient-focused and evidence-based but that didn't meet best practices as the art and science of plain language evolved.

"We had to prioritize our efforts," says Baker. "And then we created a training program for the Content Team and a communication strategy to explain to all employees what we were doing and how it would help people."

What problems did Healthwise focus on first?

Training was a big first step. "We hired a plain language trainer to teach us, and we sent one of our associate editors to plain language boot camp," says Baker. "We committed to using plain language best practices on all new content. And we began to use more visual content, and eventually videos, to tell the story."

 Center for Plain Language

The team built a *Plain Language Glossary*, which continues to expand. They also started a project affectionately called "PLing," for "plain languaging." That meant tackling existing content to bring it in line with the company's new focus on plain language.

Talking about the effort helped clear communication become part of the company's brand and culture.

Launching a User Experience (UX) Team was also critical to success. The team provides research, user-centered design, and testing. They also created easy-to-use visual, interactive, and video content.

 **PROGRESS**

How did Healthwise educate writers to understand technical and complex subject matter and communicate well with technical folks?

Writing about diseases and conditions often means taking a very difficult subject and "translating" it into plain English. Many content developers at Healthwise have hands-on experience, as nurses or physical therapists, for example. Each understands not only his or her subject area but also what's important for people to know. And others on the team are especially skilled at translating that information clearly.

How did Healthwise engage graphic designers to ensure an easy-to-understand message?

Graphic designers on the Healthwise UX Team work closely with writers, subject matter experts, and editors.

"Everyone here recognizes that being clear is not just about the words," says Baker. "Design and visual elements affect how well someone can understand information."

So does the choice and variety of the medium. Sometimes video is the best way to communicate. So designers and producers are integral to the content development process.

To what degree did a fear of "dumbing down" slow progress, and how did you address this?

"We heard the 'dumbing down' fear, but only a little," says Baker. "When you explain that most people prefer information that's easy to understand, and that health information in particular is often not clear, it's hard to argue against simplicity.

 Center for Plain Language

"Almost everyone has had an experience where their ability to understand something their doctor said, or to make a decision, was compromised. This is often due to the complex language. But pain, worry, anxiety, side effects of medicines, lack of sleep, these all make it hard to focus on the news or message related to our health.

"So why not make all the information as clear as possible, for everyone, all the time? And then, when you test two versions of content and prove that people prefer the plainer one, that's powerful."

How did Healthwise keep the program alive over the long term?

At Healthwise, plain language is more than a program, it's a commitment. The company continues all the work it has done in the past, like training, and changes and adapts as they learn more and get more feedback, which is constantly.

Karen states, "We added the 3Ps—plain, personal, possible—to our content development process to reflect our focus on helping each person understand their health so they can do what they can for themselves, in a way that's right for them."

Healthwise also has to make sure the companies that use its content understand the importance of plain language. They do this through presentations, blogs, and trainings. Then the Healthwise team shares the results of its consumer testing to keep plain language alive and real.

Was there an enforcement component?

At Healthwise, plain language skills are noted in job descriptions and performance reviews for many positions.

Does Healthwise reward those who do a great job using plain language?

Healthwise recognizes and rewards employees who excel at plain language, to encourage the employee and others, and to work to spread the news about plain language across the company.

Healthwise uses its Plain Language Bulletin to showcase its best work. Those who demonstrate the highest skills also receive commendations in their annual appraisals as well as in pay raises based on performance.

Feedback from clients is shared at all-staff meetings. And when Healthwise wins national recognition for plain language efforts, they celebrate as a company. In 2010, Healthwise won the first Grand ClearMark Award from the Center for Plain Language. They have won other awards in subsequent years. To share this good news and celebrate the employees who contributed, Healthwise describes the winning entry and features the employees' names in their internal newsletter.

Center for Plain Language

OUTCOMES

Did Healthwise meet its initial goals, and if so, how did it know?

Baker says "The best metric is the ongoing success of Healthwise.

"We deliver a host of digital, interactive, and print products to top health plans, hospitals, physician groups, and consumer health websites," she says. "Twenty-five percent of doctors in the U.S. can prescribe our content to patients through their electronic medical records. And over the past 41 years, people have used our content and tools more than 1.5 billion times."

Healthwise attributes its success to being true to its mission. The commitment to plain language better enables Healthwise to help people make better health decisions.

Did Healthwise add other goals?

New goals make the organization better. Baker recently worked with the Legal Team to rewrite a license agreement in plain language.

What positive comments did Healthwise receive from its staff or from customers?

Employees at Healthwise are proud of their efforts and continued success. They use the content themselves and for their families. And everyone at the Idaho-based organization can tell you what plain language means.

Externally, the commitment to plain language is a differentiator for the company in the market. Clients need and expect content providers to use plain language for many reasons:

⇒ More people are aging and need health information.

⇒ With an aging population can come multiple chronic conditions.

⇒ More people have health insurance who didn't have it before, and they need to understand and manage much of their own care.

Any negative reaction?

Occasionally, someone with a medical degree or scientific background quibbles over the tension between plainness and precision. When faced with this concern, Healthwise repeats a basic tenet: accuracy is nonnegotiable. "It's why our clients and their patients trust Healthwise," says Baker.

How many people are involved now (as opposed to at the start)?

The Content Team today includes more than forty people. UX is about twenty-strong. But all employees are involved to some extent in plain language work. That's as true today as when the founder introduced the concept in 1975.

Does plain language feel like part of Healthwise's culture, or are you still working on that?

Plain language is unquestionably part of the Healthwise culture and brand.

What are Healthwise's goals/plans for the future?

Healthwise is in the midst of a big project to structure content so that it can be used, and reused, across different products. As writers structure content, they have an additional chance to "PLing" the content. They find and craft the best ways to describe concepts. Then that language can be used in multiple places.

What advice would Healthwise give an organization looking to start its own program?

Here is Baker's list of advice for starting a plain language program where you work:

- ⇒ Find a champion in your leadership.
- ⇒ Assess where you are in your current state.
- ⇒ Train. And keep training.
- ⇒ Know your audience.
- ⇒ Recognize that it's not just about the words.
- ⇒ Involve/ask/test with your end users.

Center for Plain Language

Plain Language and Clear Communication Resources

WEBSITES

Center for Plain Language
www.centerforplainlanguage.org

Plain Language Act | Office of the Director of National Intelligence
http://www.dni.gov/index.php/resources/plain-language-act

The Plain Language Action and Information Network (PLAIN)
www.plainlanguage.gov

Plain Language Association InterNational (PLAIN)
www.plainlanguagenetwork.org

Plain Language | National Institutes of Health (NIH)
http://www.nih.gov/institutes-nih/nih-office-director/office-communications-public-liaison/clear-communication/plain-language

Plain Language | Office of Personnel Management (OPM)
https://www.opm.gov/information-management/plain-language

Plain Language | Center for Disease Control and Prevention – Health Literacy
http://www.cdc.gov/healthliteracy/developmaterials/plainlanguage.html

Plain Language | U.S. Department of Health and Human Services
http://health.gov/communication/literacy/plainlanguage/PlainLanguage.htm

Plain Writing | Social Security Administration
https://www.ssa.gov/agency/plain-language

For more options, do a Google search on the words "plain language" and "clear communication." In the meantime, these should keep you busy.

BOOKS

Lifting the Fog of Legalese: Essays on Plain Language (Joe Kimble)
Combines the strong evidence and myth-busting arguments for plain legal language with much practical advice and many useful examples. And no other book is more likely to open lawyers' eyes to the emptiness of legalese.

 Center for Plain Language

Writing for Dollars, Writing to Please: The Case for Plain Language in Business, Government and Law (Joe Kimble)
Presents return on investment (ROI) examples and empirical evidence for using plain language. It has been described as "the one we've been waiting for" and "a game-changer for public communication."

Plain English for Lawyers, 5th Edition (Richard Wydick)
Still one of the best books about plain language, written for lawyers but useful to everyone.

Legal Writing in Plain English; A Text with Exercises, 4th Edition (Bryan Garner)
Sets a new standard for plain legal writing and is very readable by non-lawyers. It covers all the most important plain language techniques.

Writing in Plain English (Robert Eagleson)
Developed for public servants, this book provides a step-by-step guide to planning, writing, designing, and testing documents.

Plain Language for Lawyers (Michelle Asprey)
Another excellent book targeted at legal writing, this one from Australia.

Oxford Guide to Plain English (Martin Cutts)
Completely updated, including expanded word lists, new words, clichés to avoid, and recent real-life examples.

Writing Readable Regulations (Tom Murawski)
57 ways to boost compliance and strengthen enforcement by helping readers find provisions quickly, understand them easily, and act on them confidently.

JOURNALS

Clarity is an international group of lawyers and lay people interested in supporting clear legal language. Previous issues of the journal Clarity are available online. Contact Joe Kimble at *kimblej@cooley.edu* for membership information.

The Scribes Journal of Legal Writing periodically publishes articles on plain language. Tables of contents for previous issues are online.

The Michigan Bar Journal publishes a regular column on plain language. Some recent articles include: "Strike 3 for Legalese" (PDF), "The Plain Writing Act of 2010" (PDF), and "Writing to Persuade Judges" (PDF).

Center for Plain Language

HANDBOOKS

Federal Plain Language Guidelines (U.S.)
Guidelines with examples from the federal working group.

Drafting Legal Documents
US Office of the Federal Register, which publishes all federal regulations.

A Plain English Handbook (SEC)
Written for the finance industry but useful to all.

Center for Plain Language

About the E-Book Project Team

DONNA M. CREASON, EXECUTIVE EDITOR

Donna is a writer, author, and certified technical communicator with a two-decade career in communications, publishing, training development and design, content management, and computer information systems. Through her own company, Donna provides design, development, and consulting services to organizations and individuals worldwide. Since 2013, she has been a guest faculty member for the Office of Personnel Management (OPM) seminar *Effective Writing in the Federal Government.* For these seminars, she provides instructor and editorial services on topics such as: The Plain Writing Act of 2010; the effective use of language; exploring outlines and editing; identifying and writing to your audience; and effective e-mail communications.

BRIAN BERKENSTOCK, PROJECT COORDINATOR & CONTENT DEVELOPER/EDITOR

Brian is a writer, editor, content strategist, plain language devotee, and all-around word nerd. Brian is one of the architects of Aetna's plain language effort. And he is a board member with the Center for Plain Language.

ROBIN KILROY, CONTENT DEVELOPER/EDITOR

Robin is a Learning Advisor (Clear Communication) at the Canada School of Public Service, the training arm for the Government of Canada. She has a deep interest in clear communication, the Web and information design, and believes in sharing her knowledge and expertise with colleagues.

BETH LANDAU, CONTENT DEVELOPER/EDITOR

Beth is a freelance writer and editor with an MFA in Creative Nonfiction. She is a former English teacher and an advocate for chronically ill students. Clear communication has always been Beth's focus. Her series about "Gender Dysphoria" was a ClearMark Award of Distinction finalist in early 2016.

LISA VAN ALSTYNE, CONTENT DEVELOPER/EDITOR

Lisa is the Chief of the Branch of Policy, U.S. Fish & Wildlife Service, Wildlife & Sport Fish Restoration Program (WSFR). Since joining WSFR six years ago, she has helped the Service toward the goal of applying clear/plain language to regulations, Service Manual chapters, and guidance. This approach has led to less confusion, increased consistency, and clearly defining responsibilities and expectations—all of which helps WSFR to better achieve its conservation mission. Lisa is the primary author of 50 CFR 86— Boating Infrastructure Grant Program, Proposed rule that received a ClearMark award in the Legal category in 2013. Prior to coming to work for the Service, Lisa worked for

Center for Plain Language

New York State for 29 years, combining her passions for writing and the environment. In various capacities of state service, she produced content for environmental education, websites, and targeted projects.

PAT TRUMAN, PROOFREADER
Through relentless, good-catch proofreading, Pat advocates for consumers of healthcare information from her role as Associate Editor at Healthwise in Boise, Idaho. In previous careers, she won semiconductor process engineers over with the use of plain language, and she convinced previously skeptical sixth-graders that writing and self-editing are cool.

Center for Plain Language

Four Ways to Support the Center of Plain Language

BECOME A MEMBER

Members receive special pricing on workshops, awards nomination fees, and events. Best of all, they get to show their support of the Center and plain language. Join now.

SPONSORSHIP

Since 2010, the ClearMark Awards have recognized the best in clear communications from across the public, private, and nonprofit sectors.

Our annual Awards ceremony at the National Press Club garners significant media attention and brings together plain language supporters from around the country. We accept nominations from across North America, expanding our reach and celebration of the best plain language content.

As a ClearMark sponsor, you'll showcase your commitment to plain language and promote clarity for all—at America's premier plain language event. Ready to become a sponsor?

MAKE A DONATION

As a donor, your contribution goes to support our core activities and events, including legislative advocacy, federal compliance reporting, awards, and professional workshops. ***Donations are 100% tax deductible, in contrast to memberships and sponsorships.*** Make a donation.

VOLUNTEER

We are also always looking for a few good volunteers. You can participate in any of our initiatives. Become a volunteer.

 Center for Plain Language

CPSIA information can be obtained
at www.ICGtesting.com
Printed in the USA
BVOW07s1600220817
492765BV00018B/37/P